Therapy Dogs:

Compassionate Modalities

Therapy Dogs:

Compassionate Modalities

Kris Butler

Funpuddle Publishing Associates

Published by
Funpuddle Publishing Associates
12201 Buckskin Pass
Norman, OK 73026

ISBN 0-9747793-1-8
Therapy Dogs: Compassionate Modalities
Book only

ISBN 0-9747793-2-6
Therapy Dogs: Compassionate Modalities
Book with DVD

Table of Contents

Therapy Dogs:

Compassionate Modalities

Setting the Stage

NOTES

From the Author

This book contains important information beyond what is covered in the DVD. I think you'll find it useful to use the book as you view the DVD, and then to refer back to the DVD as you study the book further.

DVD running time is approximately 46 minutes. The DVD contains an introduction to the important roles associated with every animal-enhanced intervention. Then, seven vignettes follow. After each vignette, two lists appear. The first list identifies the skills demonstrated by the dog you have just seen. The lists of canine skills are intended to help dog trainers and instructors prepare their clients to participate in similar exercises. The second list following each vignette identifies specific treatment goals. The lists of patient goals are intended to increase human service providers' awareness of therapeutic possibilities associated with similar animal-enhanced exercises.

Text information that appears during the DVD is repeated in this book. Additionally, this book is interspersed with "points to ponder" – comments and clarification relating to each of the therapeutic exercises shown in vignettes throughout the DVD. The book also contains information, identified as "sidebars," about issues that are not addressed, or only cursorily addressed, during the DVD.

The DVD offers viewers very few warm and fuzzy close-up shots of the dogs. The vignettes presented on the DVD were intentionally shot from a wide angle perspective to include the dog's interactions with the patient, of course; but also to capture the important and ongoing relationship between the dog and handler, and between the handler and staff person throughout. It is my sincere hope that people who complete this book and DVD, in addition to feeling good about visiting animal programs, will be able to develop effective, goal-directed interventions that enhance treatment outcomes. I believe that this enhanced objective requires a broader view than most have held.

To accommodate viewers who want to "flip" back and forth through the DVD presentation in the same manner as readers can flip through this book, the DVD offer chapter points. Viewers may select "menu" on their DVD players' remote controls to be presented with chapter options that, when selected, will take the DVD presentation directly to designated points that correspond with this book.

The people in the DVD are acting. However, the roles they represent are vital to every animal-enhanced intervention. Throughout this book, actors are usually identified by their roles: dog, handler, staff person, or patient. Since dogs are essential components of the human-and-dog treatment teams discussed in this book, I like to refer to them using the pronoun "who," rather than the impersonal, but grammatically correct, "that."

In real life, the dogs in this presentation work *professionally* with their handler (me). They are insured through an insurance policy that covers their handler's business property and liabilities. When working professionally, handlers are neither eligible for, nor dependent upon, the volunteers' insurance that is offered by national and local therapy dog registries. Although safety remains the paramount concern, professional people covered by professional liability insurance clearly have more choices in ways to offer canine-related interactions to their clients than do volunteer handlers who are governed by therapy dog registries. Many of those broader professional options are reflected in the interventions shown throughout this DVD.

It is important for volunteers and the trainers who prepare them to understand that national therapy dog registries' insurance coverage is only for volunteers. Such coverage relates directly to compliance with a plethora of rules, which vary greatly among the various organizations.

Although I rarely use a collar or leash on my tiny dog, I did so for this DVD to give volunteer handlers that image. The limited-slip (martingale) collars on the dogs in this DVD currently are not acceptable by at least one national registry. The leashes on the dogs in this DVD would be too long for one national registry. *All* of the registries require that handlers hang onto their dogs' leashes at all times, which I intentionally choose not to do at times. One national registry currently does not insure off-leash work as is seen in the retrieving vignette. Another national registry states that its members are to provide "emotional support," and so it is questionable whether that organization would deem every interaction shown in this DVD as acceptable and insurable. For each dog and handler to best achieve long-term goals, volunteer handlers must be aware of the benefits and limitations of individual therapy dog registries.

This presentation is intended to demonstrate specific exercises you can adapt and modify to meet treatment goals in clinical settings. Readers/viewers should be aware that the environment in which these vignettes take place was structured to represent the individual therapy sessions Whisper and Meri are most accustomed to offering. If the environment were to differ from the one shown on this DVD, interventions would have to be modified to balance the environment with the handler's and dogs' talent and skill levels. People who become familiar with my first book, *Therapy Dogs Today: Their Gifts, Our Obligation* will gain a comprehensive understanding of environmental elements and issues that surround animal-enhanced interventions, including a thorough knowledge of calming signals and body language referred to throughout this book

Now, let's get started!

Cast and crew

DVD Actors
Ally Richardson, R.N., as spokes person and staff person
Karen Ninman, as patient
Kris Butler, as therapeutic animal handler
Meri and Whisper, as themselves

Meri and Whisper are family members and professional working partners of Kris Butler.

Vignettes for DVD were taped at American Dog Obedience Center's seminar facility in Norman, OK.

DVD Camera and Editing
Steve Reilly Productions, Oklahoma City

Book Editor
Randall Turk

Cover Design
Dustin Tate, Dotman Graphic Design Inc., Norman, OK

Front Cover Photo
Kris Butler

Back Cover Photo
Manda Moon

Introduction on DVD

Welcome to *Therapy Dogs: Compassionate Modalities*, a Reaching People Through Dogs program, produced by Funpuddle Publishing Associates. Reaching People Through Dogs programs have been developed by Kris Butler to introduce volunteers, educators, health care providers, and trainers to the best ways to work with dogs to increase human healing, learning, and self-awareness.

The purpose of *Therapy Dogs: Compassionate Modalities* is to introduce viewers to creative exercises that include dogs as tender, compassionate modalities in clinical and educational settings.

The key positions targeted by this presentation are the dog, the handler, and professional staff at the facilities which the dog and handler visit. Sometimes staff and handler are the same person, to whom we refer as a dual-role handler. Trainers and instructors, who play a vital secondary role, will be able to observe the skills their clients will need in order to participate in similar exercises. Each of these positions is responsible for fulfilling a specific role.

- The handler's role is to present the dog.
- The dog's role is to receive the person being visited.
- Staff's role is to facilitate the intervention.
- The trainer's role is to prepare the team to visit.

There are a number of specific tasks associated with each of these key roles. This presentation will focus on some, but not all, of those tasks. The tasks highlighted in this presentation relate to functional goals and ways to make meeting them interesting and fun for the people we serve. By motivating our clients to engage and actively participate in their therapy, we encourage success.

In presenting their dogs, handlers are responsible for positioning their dogs. This presentation will introduce positioning options that can be utilized to address a variety of treatment goals.

Positioning requires that handlers consider:
- Stages of interaction
  - during introduction
  - as dog receives person being visited
  - during closure
- Goals, as determined by staff
- Dog's comfort level

Receiving the people being visited requires that dogs demonstrate behaviors that (minimally) cause people to feel safe and secure. The dogs in this presentation are well-suited to their various tasks. We've identified specific canine behaviors to watch for – behaviors that actually enhance the therapeutic process.
- Willingness to initiate contact
- Sustained engagement
- Periods of eye contact
- Behaviors that can be redirected
- Respect for personal boundaries

During this presentation, "staff" refers to therapists, educators, and health care providers. Staff's role is to facilitate the intervention. Every intervention has at least one goal determined by staff. This presentation focuses on the task of motivating clients to meet functional goals. After each demonstration, you'll view a list of potential client goals that might be addressed through similar exercises. The list is never complete, and we challenge you to use your imagination to develop your own exercises and outcomes.

"Tools of the trade" refers to equipment used to enhance outcomes in clinical and educational environments. Equipment is matched to the population being visited and to each dog's skill and comfort levels.

By working creatively with appropriate dogs, a wide range of client goals can be addressed. Appropriate dogs, presented creatively, provide powerful incentives to people who might otherwise be reluctant to participate.

As you view the vignettes presented on the DVD, use your imagination to determine how you might include or modify these exercises to match your program.

- Handlers – Consider the combined skill, talent, and comfort levels of you and your dogs.
- Professional staff – Consider the ways you might address your patients' or students' specific goals through exercises similar to these.
- Dog trainers and instructors – Consider how you would prepare your handler clients and their dogs to participate in clinical and educational environments.

Therapy Dogs:

Compassionate Modalities

Visitation Vignette

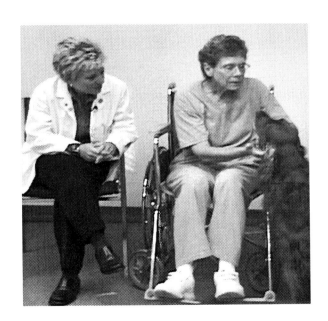

NOTES

Introduction on DVD

Every intervention begins with an introduction and ends with closure. What happens in between depends on the goals of the program. Visitations are the most common animal-enhanced programs. Handlers and their dogs provide people they visit with distraction and incentives to socialize and communicate.

Skills demonstrated by Meri

- Walking with handler
- Stand
- Stay
- Positioning skills
- Ability to respond, regardless of handler's position

GOALS ● VISITATIONS

Patient goals associated with visitations

- Activity tolerance
- Give and receive affection
- Affect
- (Decreased) Agitation
- (Decreased) Anxiety
- Appropriate touch
- Attention to task
- Confidence
- Cooperation
- Coordination (fine & gross motor)
- (Decreased) Depression
- (Decreased) Difficulty of separation from family and pets
- (Decreased) Distractibility
- Distraction from pain
- Expression
- Incentives and rewards
- Level of interest in activities
- Memory stimulation
- Motivation
- Motor planning
- Normalization activity
- Opportunity to nurture
- Orientation to reality
- Pain management
- Play and laughter
- Sense of purpose
- Range of motion
- Rapport
- Relaxation
- Reminiscing
- (Decreased) Restlessness
- Safety awareness
- Self-esteem
- Socialization
- Social skills
- Spatial relations
- Initiation of speech
- Compensatory speech strategies
- Stress reduction
- Tactile stimulation
- Validation
- Visual tracking

POINTS ● TO PONDER

Handler
- Initially stands outside of patient's personal zone while making introductions and explaining dog's presence.
- Looks to staff person for positioning preferences; then sits in a chair, putting herself at patient's level.
- Makes dog's "permission to visit" cue sound like an introduction.
- Open-ended question encourages expression. (What can you tell me about your dog?)
- Offers closure – tells patient the visit is ending.

Dog
- Remains at her handler's side during the introduction, respectful of patient's personal boundaries.
- Receives her patient by making and maintaining eye contact and remaining physically engaged with her patient.

Staff Person
- Locks the patient's wheelchair before the dog moves in.
- Gives handler clear directions regarding the best placement for the dog before, not after, the handler positions the dog.
- Talks with patient without distracting dog.

SIDEBAR ● HANDLER POSITIONING

Handlers should make every effort to position themselves at the same level as the people they visit. This might involve pulling up a chair or, if chairs are not available, squatting down. Having chairs available might require advance planning.

Handlers must work with their dogs in advance, to show them that sitting in chairs, sitting on the floor, and squatting are "normal" positions for handlers to assume. Training classes can easily accommodate future visiting dog and handler teams by including exercises that require handlers to sit in chairs, sit on the floor, squat, and kneel while working through obedience exercises and games with their dogs.

Therapy Dogs:

Compassionate Modalities

Petting and Brushing Vignette

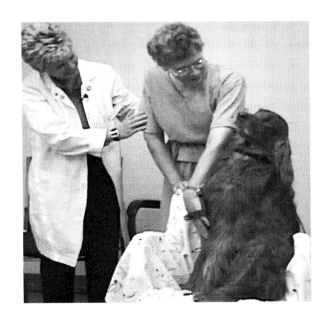

NOTES

Introduction on DVD

Some people seem to enjoy loving and nurturing exercises. Petting keeps these people engaged. Other people seem more interested in purposeful or functional tasks. Brushing or massaging the dog keeps task-oriented people engaged better than simple petting.

Savvy staff can use petting and brushing exercises to meet specific physical goals.

Savvy handlers will learn to position appropriate dogs in ways that accommodate the needs of their patients, while also considering their dogs' comfort levels.

Skills demonstrated by Meri
- Positioning skills
- Ability to respond, regardless of handler's position

GOALS ● PETTING, BRUSHING

Patient goals associated with petting, brushing

- Affect
- (Decreased) Anxiety
- Appropriate touch
- Attention to task/distractibility
- Attention span
- Balance
- Compensatory skills
- Cooperation
- Coordination
- Crossing midline
- Daily living skills
- (Decreased) Depression
- Dexterity
- (Decreased) Difficulty of separation from family and pets
- Distraction from pain
- Empowerment, control
- Endurance
- Expression
- Following directions
- Hand-eye coordination
- Identifying/naming objects
- Incentives, reward
- Motivation
- Motor integration
- Normalization activity
- Proprioception (body/space awareness)
- Providing information
- Sense of purpose
- Range of motion
- Rapport
- Relaxation
- (Decreased) Restlessness
- Sensory integration
- Spatial relations
- Strength
- Stress reduction
- Opportunity to succeed
- Tactile stimulation
- Transfer skill
- Trunk control

POINTS ● TO PONDER

Handler

- For safety, moves dog away from patient while patient transfers from wheelchair to chair.
- Repositions dog frequently, to accommodate patient.
- Presents Meri's jumping into chair prematurely as desire to visit instead of inappropriate behavior. Does not correct dog. It would have been better if handler had moved dog farther from mild confusion that surrounded placement of chair.
- While dog is in chair, drops leash and sits back, emphasizing the dog-to-patient connection.

Dog

- Remains at handler's side during introduction.
- During patient's transfer, is easily directed and repositioned by handler, away from patient.
- Receives her patient by appearing eager to visit, demonstrating eye contact, leaning back toward patient (while in chair), and remaining engaged.
- Is respectful of patient's personal boundaries.

Staff Person

- Uses patient's eagerness to visit with dog to motivate patient to practice transfer skills.
- Informs handler of intent to transfer patient to chair *before* handler positions dog.
- Gives handler clear directions about dog's placement.
- Uses brushing to address more complex goals.
- Attends carefully to patient while handler manages dog.
- Does not interact with dog in any way that would draw dog's attention away from patient.

21

SIDEBAR ● DOGS IN CHAIRS

Placing dogs up into chairs can be an effective positioning technique. It creates a greater sense of intimacy, makes dogs more reachable, and increases dogs' abilities to focus on patients by reducing the environmental distractions available to dogs. Medium-size dogs, too large to sit in patients' laps, can be difficult for people in chairs to reach when these dogs are on the floor. Being positioned up in chairs helps appropriate medium-size dogs to better receive the people they are visiting. People in beds might have trouble reaching, or even seeing, dogs who are standing on the floor. Positioning skills that enable dogs to visit comfortably from chairs can provide extremely rewarding setups when patients are confined to their beds.

However, there are important ethical considerations. Handlers must be aware that requiring their dogs to stay in chairs creates a sense of being "cornered." A dog in a chair is virtually trapped. Some dogs are not comfortable visiting from chairs.

Handlers must continually watch for communication that signals discomfort. Training should include assurances to dogs that, if their discomfort reaches a point that they want to get down, they will be allowed to do so. No dog should be forced to assume or remain in this vulnerable position. The number of people who surround a dog in a chair should be limited. People standing tend to cause more stress to dogs than seated people. Note that throughout this and other vignettes, Meri's chair is purposely positioned with the open end facing out, so that it is apparent to Meri that it is her choice to remain there – or not.

Therapy Dogs:

Compassionate Modalities

Dressing the Dog Vignette

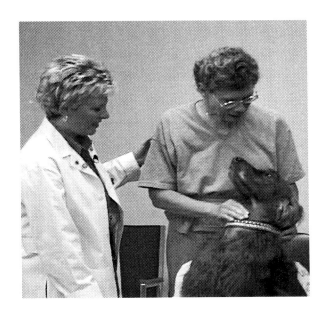

NOTES

Introduction on DVD

Putting equipment on a dog is referred to as "dressing the dog." Like brushing, dressing provides patients with practical and functional physical tasks. Additionally, positioning the equipment and managing buckles and snaps provide patients with opportunities for solving problems. There is a starting point and a stopping point. The dog being dressed equals success.

Handlers depend on staff for subtle cues as to each patient's ability. If the harness is too complicated, or if time is limited, the handler introduces a collar. If buckling the collar is an appropriate exercise, the handler requests patient to do so. If buckling the collar is beyond patient's capabilities, the handler buckles the collar and hands it to the patient to slide over the dog's head. Patients who are able snap the second leash onto the dog's second collar or harness. Handlers accommodate patients who are not able to dress the dog.

Skills demonstrated by Meri
- Sit
- Stand
- Stay
- Positioning skills

GOALS ● DRESSING DOG

Patient goals associated with dressing dog

- Activity tolerance
- Attention to task/distractibility
- Balance
- Cause and effect
- Compensation for visual field cut
- Confidence level
- Cooperation
- Coordination (fine and gross motor)
- Daily living skills
- Decision making
- Distraction from pain
- Empowerment, control
- Endurance
- Eye-hand coordination
- Following instructions
- Frustration tolerance
- (Decreased) Hyperactivity
- Identifying/naming objects
- Incentives and rewards
- Independence
- Language development
- Leisure skills
- Motor planning
- Normalization activity
- Problem solving
- Proprioception (body/space awareness)
- Sense of purpose
- Ability to organize
- Range of motion
- Rapport
- Self-esteem
- Sensory integration
- Sequencing
- Spatial relations
- Speech
- Strength (may add arm weights)
- Opportunity to succeed
- Tactile stimulation
- Trunk control

POINTS ● TO PONDER

Handler
- Uses activity the patient desires (walking) to motivate patient to work on other skills.
- Uses chair to make dog more accessible to patient and to create a greater sense of intimacy.
- Looks to staff person for a signal as to whether or not patient can buckle collar before offering instructions to patient.
- Gives patient clear instructions to follow.
- Keeps dog's attention on handler instead of on patient while patient works with equipment.
- Encourages patient to express a connection between this therapy and daily living activities.

Dog
- Is easily and willingly repositioned.
- Receives her patient by making eye contact and remaining engaged.

Staff Person
- Is aware of handler's need for direction regarding patient's ability to buckle collar, and responds subtly to handler.
- Positions and repositions patient to meet a wide variety of patient goals.

SIDEBAR ● DUAL-ROLE HANDLERS

Educators and human service providers who work with their own dogs within their professional environments are referred to by this author as "dual-role handlers." They are their dogs' handlers and advocates (one role) and they are staff (another distinct role) – both in one human package. The attention required to fulfill the role of primary staff person leaves less attention available for the dog-handler role during interventions. Try to imagine the staff person in each of these vignettes also serving as Meri's or Whisper's handler.

Dual-role handlers require dogs who are able to fill any voids left by their multi-tasking handlers. Dogs who work with dual-role handlers must be skilled to the degree that they behave appropriately even in the absence of direct handler attention. It is important that dogs who work with dual-role handlers possess specific skills and talents for the purpose of meeting specific patient or student goals. Because dual-role handlers might not enjoy the option of switching environments or changing targeted populations, it is important they consider the selection and training of their dogs especially carefully.

Therapy Dogs:

Compassionate Modalities

Walking the Dog Vignette

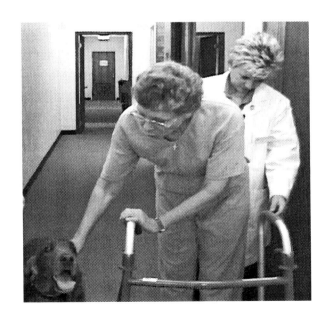

NOTES

Introduction on DVD

Time and time again, patients who have been reluctant to walk have changed their minds when offered the opportunity to walk with a dog.

Walking with patients is a high-level exercise that requires careful staff planning and exemplary dog and handler skills.

When possible, walking follows the patient's successfully "dressing" the dog with a harness or second collar and second leash. If patients are not capable of dressing the dog, the handler should nonchalantly prepare the dog to walk.

Note the careful setup with the handler in control of the dog and staff person's careful attention to the patient and to the environment. Environmental planning is essential. Note how much room is required.

Skills demonstrated by Meri

- Heeling, reliable to a high degree
- Ability to walk on either side of patient
- Ability to walk safely at any speed
- Ability to walk safely, close to equipment
- Reliability while moving in the midst of several people, through distractions
- Stand
- Stay
- Positioning skills

GOALS ● WALKING DOG

Patient goals associated with walking dog

- Activity tolerance
- (Decreased) Anxiety
- Attention to task/distractibility
- Balance
- Cause and effect
- Compensatory skills
- Confidence
- Cooperation
- Coordination
- Crossing midline
- Daily living skills
- Decision making
- (Decreased) Depression
- Distraction from pain
- Empowerment, control
- Endurance
- Follow directions
- Gait training
- Incentive and reward
- Mobility
- Motivation
- Motor planning
- Normalization activity
- Posture
- Problem solving
- Providing information
- Sense of purpose
- Rapport
- Relaxation
- Safety awareness
- Self-esteem
- Spatial relations
- Initiation of speech
- Intelligibility of speech
- Strength
- Opportunity to succeed
- Trunk/shoulder stabilization
- Visual perception

Handler
- Gives clear directions to patient.
- Redirects patient's holding of leash to increase safety.
- Allows dog to shift position slightly to increase dog's comfort level (while getting leashes adjusted).
- Uses frequent, subtle cues to direct and reassure dog.

Dog
- Demonstrates temporary, mild discomfort by offering calming signals initially as handler, patient and staff person stand over her in a small area, adjusting equipment.
- Receives her patient, even while walking, by making eye contact; engages patient appropriately by not making physical contact with patient or equipment.
- Looks to handler for reassurance.

Staff Person
- Carefully attends to patient.
- Helps dog remain focused on patient by maintaining an unobtrusive presence.

This page intentionally left blank.

Therapy Dogs:

Compassionate Modalities

Retrieving Vignette

NOTES

Introduction on DVD

Retrieving exercises can be extremely fun, functional, and rewarding. Physical, language, cognitive and psychosocial goals can easily be addressed through this one complex exercise.

Clearly, retrieving exercises can be risky. Dogs, handlers, staff, patients and environmental setups must all be carefully assessed to determine whether or not each is appropriate for this complicated activity.

Skills demonstrated by Meri

Retrieving requires an advanced skill level. Basic skills must be reliable to a high degree, off-leash.
- Controlled retrieve to hand
- Response and delivery to person other than handler
- Stay
- Controlled, appropriate movement through environment
- Exemplary positioning skills
- Ability to respond, regardless of handler's position

GOALS ● RETRIEVING

Patient goals associated with retrieving

- Activity tolerance
- Affect
- (Decreased) Anxiety
- Attention to task/distractibility
- Balance
- Cause and effect
- Compensatory tasks
- Complex motor planning
- Confidence
- Cooperation
- Coordination (fine &gross motor)
- Decision-making
- (Decreased) Depression
- Distraction from pain
- Empowerment, control
- Endurance
- Expression
- Following directions
- Gait training
- Identifying/naming objects
- Incentive and reward
- Language development
- Leisure skills
- Memory
- Motivation
- Motor integration
- Normalization activity
- Posture
- Play and laughter
- Problem solving
- Sense of purpose
- Range of motion
- Rapport
- Retention/ability to recall
- Safety awareness
- Self-esteem
- Sensory integration
- Sequencing
- Spatial relations
- Initiation of speech
- Intelligibility of speech
- Compensatory speech strategies
- Speech, voice projection
- Strength
- Opportunity for success
- Tactile stimulation
- Trunk control

POINTS ● TO PONDER

Handler
- Introduces a complex exercise as a game.
- Gives clear directions to patient.
- Subtly keeps dog interested when patient is not interacting with dog.
- Maintains a connection with dog through physical and verbal contact.
- Uses subtle cues to direct dog.
- Re-attaches leash as staff helps patient to stand.
- Positions dog in chair prior to first (standing) retrieve, to allow patient to experience dog at this physical level.
- Note safety issues addressed by handler throughout this exercise.

Dog
- Possesses appropriate skills for this high-level task.
- Is easily repositioned a number of times.
- Responds quickly to handler cues.
- Receives patient by making eye contact, engaging contact with patient (even laying head in patient's lap), responding. enthusiastically to patient's verbal cues, respecting patient's personal boundaries (does not lick face).
- Remains engaged during explanation period with little encouragement from patient.

Staff person
- Positions patient to meet various treatment goals.
- Assists handler in positioning dog by getting chair (duck blind).

Pro-active handlers anticipate what they think, know, or fear might happen next and act accordingly, before "it" happens. Reactive handlers respond to whatever just happened. Dogs are more comfortable when their handlers behave pro-actively. Reactive handlers create stress in their dogs.

During this vignette, on the first retrieve up into a chair, Meri let go of her retrieved item before being asked to do so by the patient. Beyond a mere infraction of the "obedience rules," retrieving dogs dropping their toys denies patients opportunities to use their affected arms and hands. Because Meri let go prematurely, the patient lost an opportunity to recall and speak a specific word to cue Meri.

Notice that Meri's handler barely responded, merely acknowledging "Meri dropped it," so the patient would not feel responsible. Meri's handler did not appear to address the issue with Meri at all during the intervention. However, in subsequent retrieves, Meri's handler became more proactive, encouraging Meri to "hold it" as the dog approached the chair to deliver her toy to the patient. Meri held the toy from that point on, and the result was success for everyone.

Handlers must become comfortable with techniques for redirecting their dogs without using noticeable corrections during interventions. Any dog's continued inability to demonstrate desired behaviors in a visiting environment is a sure sign that the team needs further training together -- but not while they are visiting. The most important thing dogs bring into clinical environments is a sense of safety and security, an intimate connection that might be shattered by a handler who felt that acknowledging some degree of imperfection in her dog's performance was more important than the healing journey taking place.

Therapy Dogs:

Compassionate Modalities

Floor Exercises Vignette

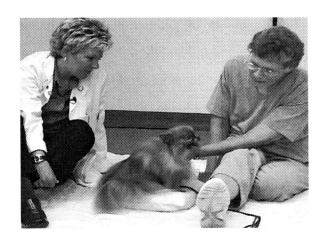

NOTES

Introduction on DVD

Floor (or bench) exercises can incorporate any combination of the activities shown so far – visiting, petting, brushing, dressing the dog, or preparing to walk the dog. The difference is in the goals set for the patient by professional staff.

When working with pediatric patients, working on the floor can be more comfortable and create a greater sense of intimacy.

Skills demonstrated by Meri and Whisper

- Moving with handler (Meri)
- Stand (Meri)
- Down (both)
- Stay (both)
- Positioning (both)
- Recall (both)

GOALS ● FLOOR EXERCISES

Patient goals associated with floor exercises

- Activity tolerance
- Affect
- Appropriate touch
- Attention to task/distractibility
- Balance reaction
- Cause and effect
- Compensatory skills for visual field cut
- Cooperation
- Coordination – fine and gross motor
- Daily living skills
- Decision-making
- (Decreased) Depression
- Distraction from pain
- Empowerment, control
- Endurance
- Expression
- Following directions
- Flexibility
- Identifying/naming objects
- Incentives and reward
- Kneeling balance
- Memory
- Motivation
- Motor integration
- Normalization activity
- Problem solving
- Providing information
- Sense of purpose
- Rapport
- Range of motion
- Relaxation
- Retention/ability to recall
- Sensory integration
- Sequencing
- Spatial relations
- Initiation of speech
- Intelligibility of speech
- Compensatory speech strategies
- Stamina
- Strength
- Stress reduction
- Opportunity for success
- Visual perception
- Visual tracking

Handler

- Keeps Meri away until patient is safely on the floor, and then moves in with dog. Waiting until patients are positioned on the floor is more comfortable for dogs because it prevents people from hovering over and dropping down upon dogs.
- Moves Meri out of the way, again, when patient is changing to kneeling position.
- Repositions Meri out of the posture that suggests dog is sublimating herself.
- Gives patient useful information about harness placement.
- Remains somewhat apart from Whisper, to help the dog focus on patient.
- Uses pillow to redirect Whisper and limit her ability to roam on the floor.

Dog – Meri

- Responds to handler's subtle cues.
- Demonstrates that, at this point in a long day of movie-making, she's had about enough. She responds to her handler, but demonstrates little interest in her patient. Meri's behavior during previous vignettes suggests that her reception of her patient during this vignette is not her normal behavior. She will receive her patient by lying down next to the patient, but that is about all. She offers calming signals - she licks her lips and initially rolls over, beyond making herself comfortable. When asked, Meri does reposition herself willingly. However, during the harness portion of this vignette, in the standing position, her tail is droopy and her body seems tense.

45

Dog – Meri (cont.)

- If this had been a real visit, there would be no mention of taking a walk after the harness was on the dog. Rather, I would have called it a day and taken Meri home. Certainly, Meri's behavior is not "bad" during this vignette; but her behavior clearly indicates she is no longer comfortable being active.

Dog – Whisper

- Receives her patient by making eye contact and soliciting patient's attention.
- Responds well to handler's cues.

Staff Person

- Attentive to patient.
- Physically pulls away from Whisper to help Whisper focus better on the patient.

Therapy Dogs:

Compassionate Modalities

Small Dog Vignette

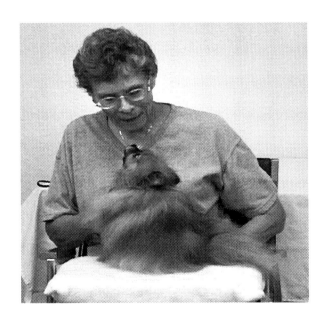

NOTES

Introduction on DVD

No matter how people might feel about large dogs, the fact remains, there are simply places a little dog can go – figuratively and literally – where a large dog might not sometimes be welcome.

Some people are more receptive to Whisper's solicitous charms than those of her larger counterparts. The patient goals remain the same, but we've developed exercises especially for Whisper, to enable her to motivate people to meet those functional goals.

Skills demonstrated by Whisper

- Stay
- Automatic stay (on pillow)
- Positioning skills

GOALS ● SMALL DOG EXERCISES

Patient goals associated with small dog exercises

- Activity tolerance
- Ambulation
- (Decreased) Anxiety
- Appropriate touch
- Attention span
- Balance
- Balance reaction
- Compensatory skills
- Cooperation
- Coordination – fine and gross motor
- Crossing midline
- (Decreased) Depression
- Distraction from pain
- Endurance
- Expression, affect
- Gait training
- Hand-eye coordination
- Hyperactivity
- Identification, naming of objects
- Inattention, neglect – right or left side
- Incentives and rewards
- Language development
- Level of interest
- Memory
- Mobility
- Motivation
- Motor integration
- Motor planning, complex motor planning
- Normalization activity
- Opportunity to succeed
- Orientation to reality
- Pain management
- Play and laughter
- Posture
- Proprioception (body/space awareness)
- Providing information
- Range of motion
- Rapport
- Recall
- Relaxation
- Reminiscing
- Restlessness
- Retention
- Sensory integration
- Decreased feelings of separation from family and pets
- Socialization
- Spatial relationships
- Speech – compensatory speech strategies
- Speech – initiation of speech
- Speech – intelligibility
- Stamina
- Strength
- Stress reduction
- Trunk control
- Trunk, shoulder stabilization
- Visual perception
- Visual tracking

POINTS ● TO PONDER

Handler
- Positions herself at the other end of the table, away from Whisper, to enhance the perception of a patient-to-dog connection.
- Does not hang onto leash, further removing the perception of her presence during interventions, to increase sense of intimacy between patient and dog.
- Explains to patient what is about to happen *before* putting pillow in patient's lap.

Dog
- Is more focused on patient in this vignette than she was during the floor vignette, due to dog's restricted movement here.
- Possesses specific skill to safely participate in table exercises.
- On the table, uses calming lip licks to acknowledge person standing over her in her intimate zone, but remains comfortable and attentive to patient.
- Receives her patient by soliciting attention, sustained eye contact and engagement.

Staff Person
- Purposefully does not hover over dog or table in order to increase dog's comfort level and ability to focus on patient
- Withdraws a step or two (handler does, too) from dog and patient when patient is sitting in chair with Whisper. There should have been chairs arranged in advance for staff person and handler, but there were not. Squatting down next to Whisper and the patient might have drawn Whisper's attention away from patient.

Whisper's playful charm is hard to resist. By sharing enthusiasm and affection, Whisper encourages success. Her confidence seems to be contagious, and the achievements of patients who catch it can be remarkable.

Small dogs like Whisper bring with them unique intrinsic vulnerabilities that I believe are associated with being prey as well as predator. Most wild rabbits weigh more than Whisper. Predators often hover over, swoop in, grab their prey, and carry it off for consumption. I believe that nature has endowed all tiny animals, including dogs like Whisper, with an intuitive sense of the seating arrangement at nature's dinner table. In addition to a sense of the sanctity surrounding personal territory that every dog possesses, I believe Whisper's inner voice alerts her to situations that resemble hovering, swooping, and grabbing. Warranted or not, her body responds to her intuition and, as her handler, I must respond to her signals that indicate she has changed from feeling safe to feeling uncomfortable.

I structure Whisper's working environments carefully. Whisper only works on the floor when her patients and therapists sit (down) on the floor with her. Whisper is positioned on a table (up as high as a human's midsection) to initially greet patients who walk up to her. I place Whisper on her familiar pillow in the laps of already seated patients. They do not pick her up; I do. When therapists or family members stand (hover) over Whisper when she is in the lap of a seated patient, I offer them chairs that I position outside of their arms' length. I've developed friendly, positive ways to reposition people who are not our patients.

SIDEBAR ● SMALL DOGS (cont.)

Shifts in Whisper's body language are apparent later, during the Conclusion Chapter of the DVD, as Ally (spokes person) turns from Whisper and begins speaking to the camera, petting Meri, but no longer interacting with Whisper. The little dog appears to be confused by this setup. She fidgets, unsure about what she should be doing. As Ally says, "At the core of each program…" viewers can see that the camera man has moved in closer. Whisper offers a new series of calming signals at this point (licking her lips and yawning), suggesting that she feels the camera man or his camera is encroaching upon the very limited personal space she is confined to. She seems to offer fewer calming signals as the camera man pulls back.

Just as surely as Whisper carries her natural vulnerabilities into the environments in which we work, I am convinced that she trusts that I will always respect her sensitivities. If I were unwilling to respond to her, Whisper's apprehensions might be confirmed. If that happened, we would lose the confident, solicitous qualities that cause people to feel such a strong connection to her.

Parts of this sidebar are excerpted from Therapy Dogs Today: Their Gifts, Our Obligation, by Kris Butler

SIDEBAR ● THE SPECIAL PILLOW

Dogs must feel comfortable in order to receive the people they are visiting. Positioning little dogs in a manner that allows them to feel safe can be challenging. Patients often are not equipped with legs and laps that encourage little dogs to feel they are on solid ground – indeed, they are not! The solution is for handlers to build platforms that fit easily in patients' laps, upon which little dogs can visit in comfort and security.

Every little dog should have a pillow or pad that is sturdy enough so that the dog is not vulnerable to shifting legs underneath. Pillow coverings should allow dogs to feel they can dig in and enjoy steady traction. (Avoid slick coverings.) Pillows and pads must be short enough to fit within the arm rests of wheelchairs, yet not so small that they will fall down between patients' legs.

In addition to serving as lap pads, pillows can be used to send messages to small dogs that, yes indeed, they are exactly where they belong. When small dogs' special pillows are placed beside patients in beds, dogs can feel secure they have permission to be there. Pillows help keep small dogs in beds "planted" in one place. Likewise, pillows can be used to station little dogs on tables, floors, or chairs beside their patients. The exact location might be unfamiliar or daunting, but the special pillow is an old familiar friend that, along with a trusted handler, implies, "This place is safe, little dog. You belong right here."

Therapy Dogs:

Compassionate Modalities

Appendices

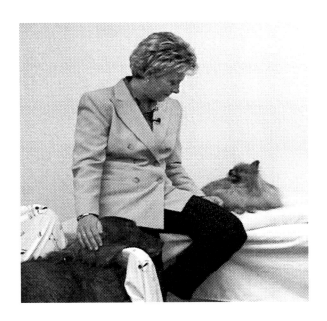

NOTES

APPENDIX 1

ABOUT THE AUTHOR

Kris Butler is a nationally recognized trainer, instructor and author. Since 1979, when she established American Dog Obedience Center in Norman, Oklahoma, her professional vision has focused on working with dogs to improve the quality of peoples' lives.

Early on, Kris turned to competitions as an outlet for her training energy. She trained and handled dogs who earned fifteen American Kennel Club (AKC) performance titles, including Companion dog (CD) and Companion Dog Excellent (CDX) obedience titles and Junior Hunter (JH) retriever hunting titles. Additionally, she coached several of her clients through AKC obedience titles with dogs she had trained for them.

These valuable experiences led Kris to seek out roles for herself and her dogs that, in addition to using her training skills, really benefited *people* as well. She directed her education and her marketing toward professional relationships that included educators and human service providers. Now she says, "I feel like the most fortunate trainer in the world every time I exit the clinical and educational 'arenas' in which my dogs and I now perform."

Beyond working with her own dogs, Kris has developed goal-directed animal-enhanced programs for therapists and special education teachers from throughout the United States. She has provided professional consulting, evaluator training, animal evaluations, and site assessment services for Delta Society in seven states. Hundreds of handlers, trainers, therapists, and educators have benefited from her "Reaching People Through Dogs" seminars. She is currently Director of International Association of Canine Professional's Therapy Dogs Division.

APPENDIX 2

GOALS FOR CLINICAL SETTINGS
A complete list of goals included in vignettes

To increase or decrease (as desired):

- Activity tolerance
- Affect, expression
- Give and receive affection
- Agitation
- Ambulation
- Anxiety
- Appropriate touch
- Attention span
- Attention to task
- Balance
- Balance reaction
- Cause and effect
- Compensatory skills
- Confidence
- Cooperation
- Coordination – fine and gross motor
- Crossing midline
- Daily living skills
- Decision making
- Depression
- Dexterity
- Distractibility
- Distraction from pain
- Empowerment, sense of control
- Endurance
- Flexibility
- Following directions
- Frustration tolerance
- Gait training
- Hand-eye coordination
- Hyperactivity
- Identification, naming of objects
- Inattention, neglect – right or left side
- Incentives and rewards
- Independence
- Kneeling balance
- Language development
- Leisure skills
- Level of interest
- Memory
- Mobility
- Motivation
- Motor integration
- Motor planning, complex motor planning
- Normalization activity
- Opportunity to nurture
- Opportunity to succeed
- Organization
- Orientation to reality
- Pain management
- Play and laughter
- Posture
- Problem solving
- Proprioception, body/space awareness
- Providing information
- Sense of purpose

- Range of motion
- Rapport
- Recall
- Relaxation
- Reminiscing
- Restlessness
- Retention
- Safety awareness
- Self-esteem
- Sensory integration
- Separation from family and pets
- Sequencing
- Socialization
- Social skills
- Spatial relationships
- Speech – compensatory speech strategies
- Speech – initiation of speech
- Speech – intelligibility
- Speech – voice projection
- Stamina
- Strength
- Stress reduction
- Transfer skill
- Trunk control
- Trunk, shoulder stabilization
- Validation
- Visual perception
- Visual tracking

APPENDIX 3

ADDITIONAL RESOURCES

Seminars, Coaching, and Mentoring
Reaching People Through Dogs Programs
Beyond Results Dog Training Services
Kris Butler
Phone 405-364-7650   www.DogsPrograms.com

National Volunteers' Registries
Therapy Dogs Incorporated
Phone 877-843-7364   www.therapydogs.com

Delta Society Pet Partners
Phone 425-226-7357   www.deltasociety.com

Therapy Dogs International, Inc.
Phone 973-252-9800   www.tdi-dog.com

Service Dogs, Assistance Dogs
Delta Society Service Dog Education Division
Phone 425-226-7357   www.deltasociety.org

International Association of Assistance Dog Partners
Phone 586-826-3938   www.iaadp.org

Therapy Dogs:

Compassionate Modalities

**Call or write or email
Funpuddle Publishing Associates
12201 Buckskin Pass, Norman OK 73026
405-364-7650
www.DogPrograms.com**

The Perfect Adjunct Text
Therapy Dogs Today
Their Gifts, Our Obligation

ISBN 0-9747793-0-X

Author Kris Butler explores the complex professional and ethical issues that surround animal-enhanced programs.

Available through the usual book-selling internet sites and at
www.DogPrograms.com